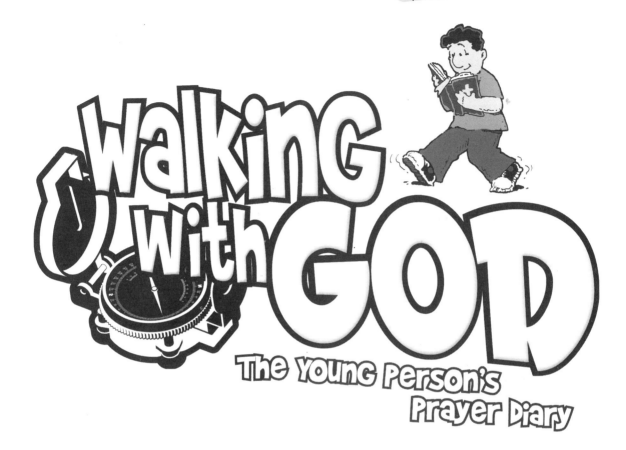

Walking With God

The Young Person's Prayer Diary

YWAM PUBLISHING

P.O. BOX 55787   SEATTLE, WA 98155

YWAM Publishing is the publishing ministry of Youth With A Mission. Youth With A Mission (YWAM) is an international missionary organization of Christians from many denominations dedicated to presenting Jesus Christ to this generation. To this end, YWAM has focused its efforts in three main areas: (1) training and equipping believers for their part in fulfilling the Great Commission (Matthew 28:19), (2) personal evangelism, and (3) mercy ministry (medical and relief work).

For a free catalog of books and materials, contact:

YWAM Publishing
P.O. Box 55787, Seattle, WA 98155
(425) 771-1153 or (800) 922-2143
www.ywampublishing.com

WalKing with God

15 14 13 12 11 10 09 08 07 06   10 9 8 7 6 5 4 3 2 1

Published by YWAM Publishing
P.O. Box 55787
Seattle, WA 98155

ISBN 0-927545-79-9

Written and compiled by Michelle Drake
Illustrations by Cheryl Knapp

Printed in the United States of America.

WELCOME!

When you walk with God, your path may take turns or become bumpy, but always keep your eyes straight ahead, looking always toward Jesus at the end of the path. He will never lead you astray.

It is my prayer that this journal will be a useful tool for you to keep your walk with God steady and always moving forward. When you look back on this journal months or years from now, you will be able to see how you have grown closer to Jesus through your daily walk with Him.

—Michelle

Proverbs 4:11-13, 25-27: I guide you in the way of wisdom and lead you along straight paths. When you walk, your steps will not be hampered; when you run, you will not stumble. Hold on to instruction, do not let it go; guard it well, for it is your life.... Let your eyes look straight ahead, fix your gaze directly before you. Make level paths for your feet and take only ways that are firm. Do not swerve to the right or the left; keep your foot from evil.

JouRNaLiNg

Keeping a journal is a priceless tool to help you walk with God every day and mark your journey. Your journal is meant to be a private place between you and God. It's a safe place to express your hopes, your dreams, your prayers, your failures, your victories, and your most private thoughts. As you write, know that God is always near you and always hears you.

You also can use the writing space to record prayers for the people and countries you learn about in this journal as well as prayers for family members and friends. As you read and study your Bible, you may want to copy into your journal a verse that is special to you and then write a few thoughts about what that verse means to you.

Your writing doesn't have to be perfect in your journal. This special journal is between you and God and no one else. Don't worry about making "mistakes" in your journal. The important thing is to write down all your thoughts.

As the days and even the years go by, you will look back on what you have written and be amazed to see how God has answered your prayers and how you have grown closer to Him through this experience of communicating with Him in your journal.

Proverbs 7:1, 3: My son, keep my words and store up my commands within you.... Bind them on your fingers; write them on the tablet of your heart.

Psalm 5:3: In the morning, O LORD, you hear my voice; in the morning I lay my requests before you and wait in expectation.

Prayer: Communicating with God

The best way to deepen your relationship with God is to spend time with Him. You can do this anytime and anywhere. Prayer is simply talking to God and listening to Him speak back to you through His Holy Spirit.

God doesn't want you to pray only when things are difficult or you have problems. He would love to hear you whisper your thoughts to Him all day long. In Matthew 7:7 Jesus says, "Ask and it will be given to you, seek and you will find." We feel closest to the people we can most easily talk to. That's why we must "practice" talking to God. Although we cannot see God, if we keep talking to Him and listening to His voice, He will show Himself to us and we will know Him better.

Although you can talk to God anywhere and anytime, it is important to set aside a time each day to read the Bible, talk to God, and quietly listen to Him speak to your heart. Choose a place that feels special to you. Perhaps a walk outside works best for you, or maybe you have a favorite chair in a quiet room. Psalm 145:18 says, "The LORD is near to all who call on him." As you go to this place each day and ask God to be near you, He will meet with you there. This will become your favorite part of the day!

John 10:27: "My sheep listen to my voice; I know them, and they follow me. I give them eternal life, and they shall never perish; no one can snatch them out of my hand."

Proverbs 8:17: "I love those who love me, and those who seek me find me."

Intercession: Praying for Others

Most of us have a hard time thinking about what is going on in other parts of the world. Sometimes we hear news reports about other countries or stories about a person's trip to another nation, but it is always difficult to imagine how people in other lands really live their daily lives. It can be tricky to pray for people in a far-off place because we don't know what their struggles are or what makes them unique.

Intercession is a fancy word for praying to God on behalf of another person. It is as if the person you are praying for is standing on one side of a bridge and God is on the other side of that bridge. You are standing in the middle of the bridge, reaching your hand across the bridge to God, asking Him to come and do something on behalf of that person. When you pray for another person or country, you become the go-between for that person and God. When you ask God for help, He actually sends out angels to do His will.

Just as you sometimes beg your parents to give you something, you can plead with God to help another person or even people in a far-off land. It is much easier to pray for yourself or your family and friends because you know what you or they need and struggle with. To pray for strangers may seem like a challenge, but it is worth it!

After reading in this journal about countries like Trinidad and Tobago, you will begin to understand the needs of the people in those countries. You can then pray for the people, using the prayer points listed for each country. God will hear your prayers, and He will begin to show you just how important and rewarding praying for others can be.

Psalm 2:8: "Ask of me, and I will make the nations your inheritance, the ends of the earth your possession."

Ezekiel 22:30: "I looked for a man among them who would build up the wall and stand before me in the gap on behalf of the land so I would not have to destroy it, but I found none."

Evangelism

When you really love someone or something, it is easy to tell others about that person or thing. Your enthusiasm continually leaks out of you. In the same way, as you get to know God more every day, it is natural to want to tell others about Him. You will find that you simply cannot help but tell others about how great God is! That's evangelism—simply telling others about God.

Often people can best understand your love for God if you share a personal experience about how He has helped you or changed your life. You can let others know about the Good News of Jesus Christ in many different ways, including reading them your favorite Bible verses or handing out gospel tracts or Bibles. Another important way you can tell others about God's love is through friendship evangelism. This is when you become involved in people's lives and your faith naturally flows out in those friendships. You might send these friends notes of encouragement with Bible verses, invite them to church, give them books that tell about God's love, or tell them that you will pray for them.

The most important part of evangelism is to let God pour out His love through you to *everyone* around you so that others visibly see Jesus in your life. Your actions can speak louder than words.

John 13:34–35: "A new command I give you: Love one another. As I have loved you, so you must love one another. By this all men will know that you are my disciples, if you love one another."

Matthew 5:13–16: "You are the salt of the earth.... You are the light of the world.... Let your light shine before men, that they may see your good deeds and praise your Father in heaven."

THE WORLD

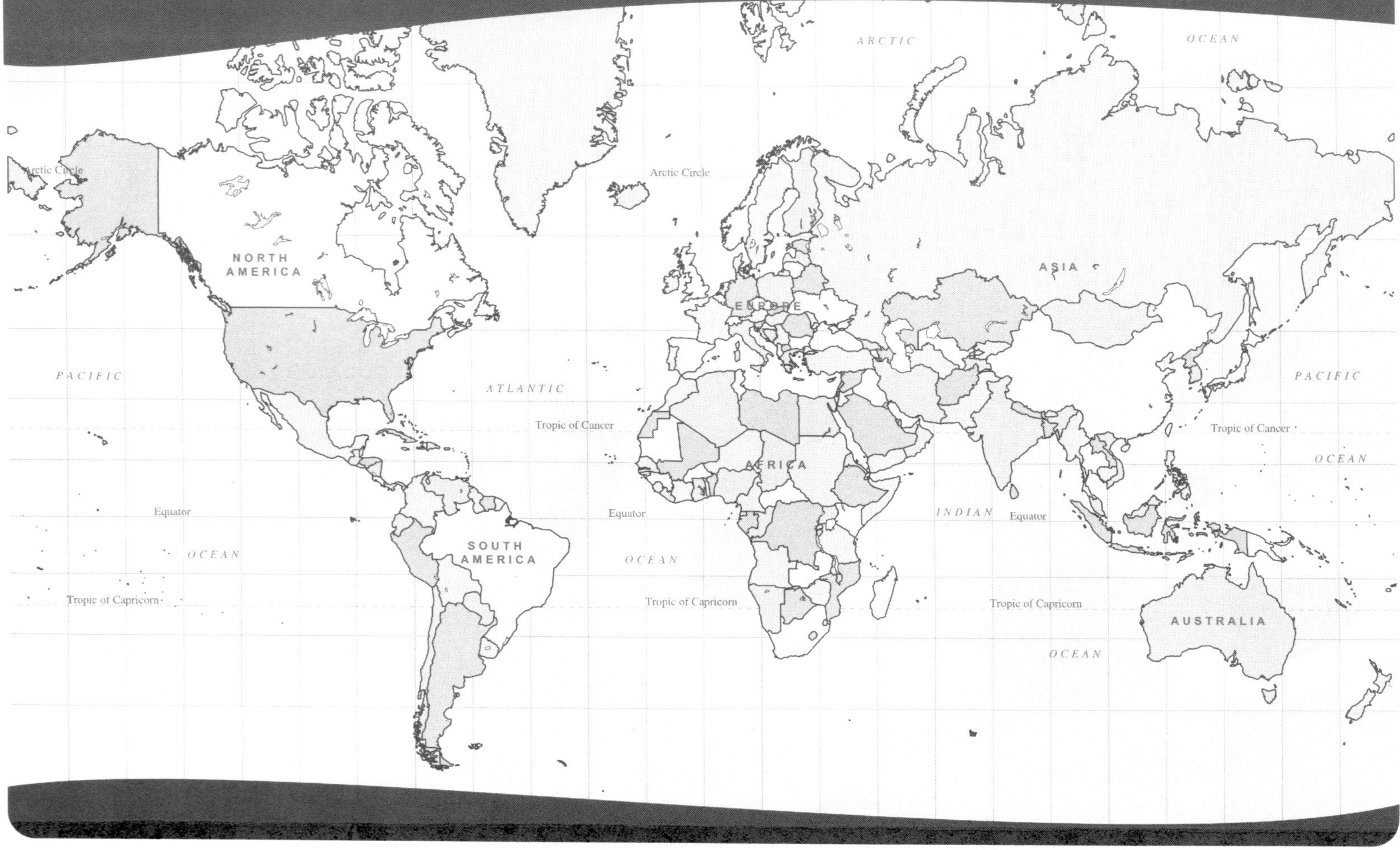

ARCTIC OCEAN

PACIFIC OCEAN

ATLANTIC OCEAN

INDIAN OCEAN

NORTH AMERICA

SOUTH AMERICA

EUROPE

ASIA

AFRICA

AUSTRALIA

Arctic Circle

Tropic of Cancer

Equator

Tropic of Capricorn

Walking with God Today

MONTH: _____   YEAR: _____

Sun	Mon	tue	wed	thu	fri	Sat

Praying for Haiti

Haiti is located on the western half of a mountainous island in the Caribbean Sea. Beautiful flamingos live in Haiti's marshy lowland lakes. The climate in Haiti is hot all year. Earthquakes, landslides, and tropical storms are common. Except for the trees on the upper mountains, most of Haiti's trees have been cut down to make room for farming.

Haiti has been described as "a country turned upside down." Most of its people's ancestors were brought to Haiti as slaves from Africa. Although slavery has ended, Haiti's people have suffered under oppressive dictatorships for more than one hundred years. Haiti is the poorest country in the Western Hemisphere, and nearly one million Haitians have left their country in hope of a better life in the U.S., Canada, Cuba, or the Bahamas.

Facing poverty and hunger every day, many Haitians eat only one small meal a day. Most Haitian children living in poverty are at least six inches shorter and fifty pounds lighter than American children of the same age. Even though most Haitians work on farms and raise crops, not enough food is grown to feed all of the people. Because running water is not available, the risk of disease from germs carried by polluted rivers and streams is high.

Thousands of Haitians live in one-room shacks made of whatever scrap materials they can find at the garbage dumps. Some areas in Haiti are so crowded that huts have been built on top of each other. Because most children work in the fields rather than go to school, 80 percent of Haitians cannot read or write. Although school is free, textbooks and other materials are not, so many families cannot afford to send their children to school.

Despite their many troubles, Haitians enjoy celebrating and dancing. The people are artistic and enjoy brightly colored paints, which they splash on their buses and buildings.

Population: 8.12 million   **Capital:** Port-au-Prince   **Languages:** French, Haitian Creole   **Religion:** Christian with a mix of voodooism (spiritism and witchcraft) 96% Bahai and other 3% Nonreligious 1%   **Average Annual Income Per Person:** $400

Pray:

- for more Haitians to be able to attend school so that they can read and write—especially so that they can read the Bible.
- that Christians will reach out to help the poor, hungry, and sick in Haiti.

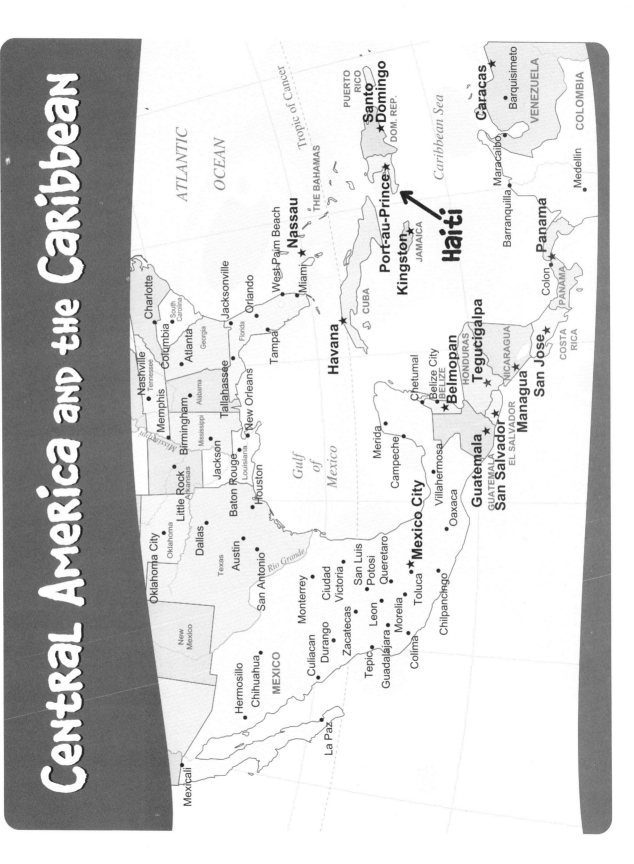

Central America and the Caribbean

Mexicali

MEXICO

Hermosillo

Chihuahua

La Paz

Culiacan

Durango

Zacatecas

Tepic

Guadalajara

Morelia

Colima

Toluca

Chilpancingo

Leon

Queretaro

San Luis Potosi

Ciudad Victoria

Monterrey

★ **Mexico City**

San Antonio

Austin

Dallas

Oklahoma City

Little Rock

Baton Rouge

Houston

New Orleans

Jackson

Birmingham

Memphis

Nashville

Charlotte

Columbia

Atlanta

Jacksonville

Orlando

Tampa

Tallahassee

West Palm Beach

Miami

New Mexico

Texas

Oklahoma

Arkansas

Louisiana

Mississippi

Alabama

Tennessee

South Carolina

Georgia

Florida

Rio Grande

Gulf of Mexico

Oaxaca

Villahermosa

Campeche

Merida

Chetumal

Belize City

BELIZE

★ **Belmopan**

★ **Guatemala**

GUATEMALA

★ **San Salvador**

EL SALVADOR

★ **Tegucigalpa**

HONDURAS

★ **Managua**

NICARAGUA

★ **San Jose**

COSTA RICA

Colon

★ **Panama**

PANAMA

Havana

★

CUBA

Nassau

★

THE BAHAMAS

ATLANTIC OCEAN

Tropic of Cancer

Kingston

★

JAMAICA

Port-au-Prince

→

Haiti

★ **Santo Domingo**

DOM. REP.

PUERTO RICO

Caribbean Sea

Maracaibo

Barranquilla

Medellin

COLOMBIA

★ **Caracas**

Barquisimeto

VENEZUELA

GReat is YOUR LOVE

Psalm 108:4 For great is your love, higher than the heavens; your faithfulness reaches to the skies.

Date	Daily Journal

Daily Journal

Date	Daily Journal

Prayer Priorities

I want to Remember in Prayer:

_____
_____
_____
_____

Date	Daily Journal

Daily Journal

Date	Daily Journal

GUARD YOUR HEART

Proverbs 4:23 Above all else, guard your heart, for it is the wellspring of life.

Date	Daily Journal

Daily Journal

Date	Daily Journal

Prayer Priorities

I want to Remember
in Prayer:

_____
_____
_____
_____

Date	Daily Journal

Daily Journal

Date	Daily Journal

I Set you apart

Jeremiah 1:5 "Before I formed you in the womb I knew you, before you were born I set you apart; I appointed you as a prophet to the nations."

Date	Daily Journal

Daily Journal

Date	Daily Journal

Prayer Priorities

I want to Remember
in Prayer:

_____

Date	Daily Journal

Daily Journal

Date	Daily Journal

Daily Journal

Date	Daily Journal

Walking with God Today

MONTH: YEAR:

SUN	MON	tue	wed	tHu	fRi	sat

PRAYING for the NetherLands

The Netherlands is a small, flat country in western Europe between Germany and Belgium. The Netherlands is often called Holland, although *Holland* actually refers to an area within the Netherlands. People in the Netherlands are called Dutch or Netherlanders.

Netherlands (or in Dutch, *Nederland*) means "low land." Long ago, the North Sea covered the country's low ground. The Dutch worked very hard to keep the water from covering their land, using windmills to pump water back to the sea and dikes (strong walls) to keep the water out. A century ago, ten thousand windmills pumped water from the country. Today, only about one thousand windmills are working.

The Netherlands is famous for its beautiful flowers, delicious cheese, and wooden shoes called *klompen* (clogs). These shoes aren't practical in the city, but farmers and fishermen still wear them when the weather is wet because they keep out dampness better than leather boots. The Netherlands is also known as the diamond center of the world. It is here that some of the world's largest and most famous diamonds are cut and polished. The Dutch have always loved art, music, dancing, painting, drama, and film. Two very famous painters, Rembrandt and Vincent van Gogh, came from the Netherlands.

The flat landscape makes the country perfect for bicycling. The Dutch ride bikes to work and for fun. Almost everyone has two bikes, one designed for long distances and one with a basket for shopping and short trips.

The Dutch like things well ordered. They feel there is a place for everything and everything has its place. They have a reputation for keeping their homes clean and tidy. One of their greatest ambitions is to have a house and a garden, and they take great pride in creating cozy homes.

Population: 16.41 million **Capitals:** Amsterdam, The Hague **Languages:** Dutch, Frisian, English **Religion:** Christian 51% Nonreligious 41% Muslim 5.5% Other 2.5%
Average Annual Income Per Person: $25,940

Pray:

- for the Dutch to return to their roots as a country that sends missionaries around the world.
- that churches will develop creative ways to reach the Dutch youth who don't seem interested in God or the church.

Europe

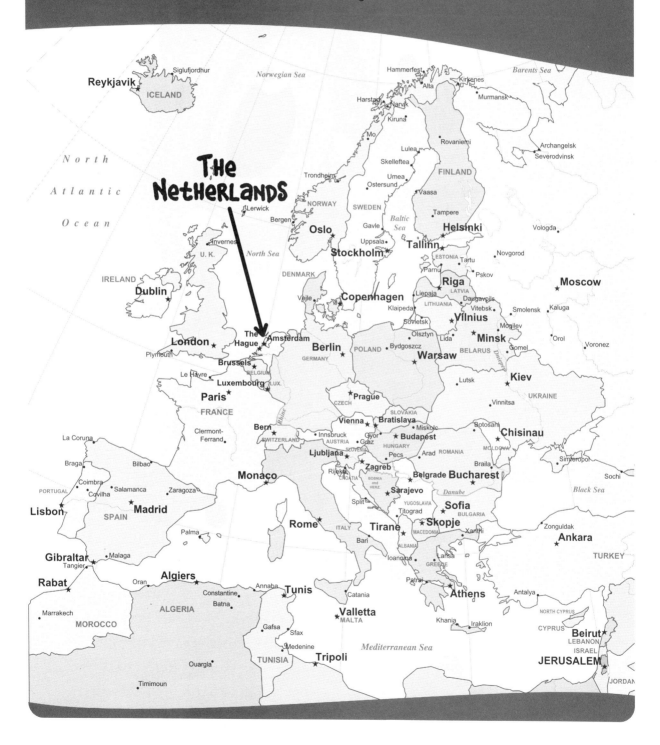

Hope and a future

Jeremiah 29:11 "For I know the plans I have for you," declares the LORD, "plans to prosper you and not to harm you, plans to give you hope and a future."

Date	Daily Journal

Daily Journal

Date	Daily Journal

Prayer Priorities

I want to Remember in Prayer:

_____

_____

_____

_____

Date	Daily Journal

Daily Journal

Date	Daily Journal

GOD REJOICES OVER YOU

Zephaniah 3:17 "The LORD your God is with you, he is mighty to save. He will take great delight in you, he will quiet you with his love, he will rejoice over you with singing."

Date	Daily Journal

Daily Journal

Date	Daily Journal

Prayer Priorities

I want to Remember in Prayer:

_____
_____
_____
_____

Date	Daily Journal

Daily Journal

Date	Daily Journal

I am the way...

JOHN 14:6 Jesus answered, "I am the way and the truth and the life. No one comes to the Father except through me."

Date	Daily Journal

Daily Journal

Date	Daily Journal

Prayer Priorities

I want to Remember
in Prayer:

_____
_____
_____
_____

Date	Daily Journal

Daily Journal

Date	Daily Journal

Daily Journal

Date	Daily Journal

Walking with God Today

MONTH: YEAR:

SUN	MON	tue	weD	thu	fri	Sat
☐	☐	☐	☐	☐	☐	☐
☐	☐	☐	☐	☐	☐	☐
☐	☐	☐	☐	☐	☐	☐
☐	☐	☐	☐	☐	☐	☐
☐	☐	☐	☐	☐	☐	☐
☐	☐	☐	☐	☐	☐	☐

Praying for Somalia

The ancient Egyptians called Somalia "God's Land." Somalia is located on a peninsula called the Horn of Africa, on the eastern coast of Africa. Most Somalis are nomads, constantly traveling through the brush and sand to find water and pastures for their herds of cattle, sheep, goats, and camels. When the water in one area dries up, the people take down their homes, load their belongings on their backs and the backs of their animals, and travel to a new location.

The Somali people have endured years of hardship from drought, famine, and war. Belonging to clans helps to give the people support and protection in a country where no law or order seems to exist. The clans are made up of extended families, so children grow up with their siblings, cousins, parents, grandparents, and aunts and uncles. Many children have not attended school for years because of the fighting and war in their country.

The most important animal to the Somalis is the camel. The most noble calling in Somalia is camel herding. The wealthier a family becomes, the more camels it will buy. Teenage boys often herd their families' camels, moving from place to place in search of water. When traveling, the boys' only food is camels' milk. Sometimes a hungry, young camel herder will drink six to ten quarts of milk a day.

Somalia has been called a "nation of poets" because of its love for poetry. The people hold contests in which poets compete to see who is the best. Until recently, the Somalis did not have a written form of poetry, so they passed their poems down verbally from generation to generation. Storytelling is an art and a tradition to the Somalis. God, daily life, camels, love, peace, and war are favorite topics in stories, poems, and songs.

Christian workers and missionaries are not currently allowed in Somalia. The small group of Christians who make up the church in Somalia must meet in private because they are in danger if their faith becomes known.

Population: 8.59 million **Capital:** Mogadishu **Languages:** Somali, Arabic **Religion:** Sunni Muslim 99.95% Christian .05% **Average Annual Income Per Person:** Unknown

Pray:

- for strength and protection for the Christian believers in Somalia.
- for food as well as the gospel to reach the many starving children in Somalia.

Africa

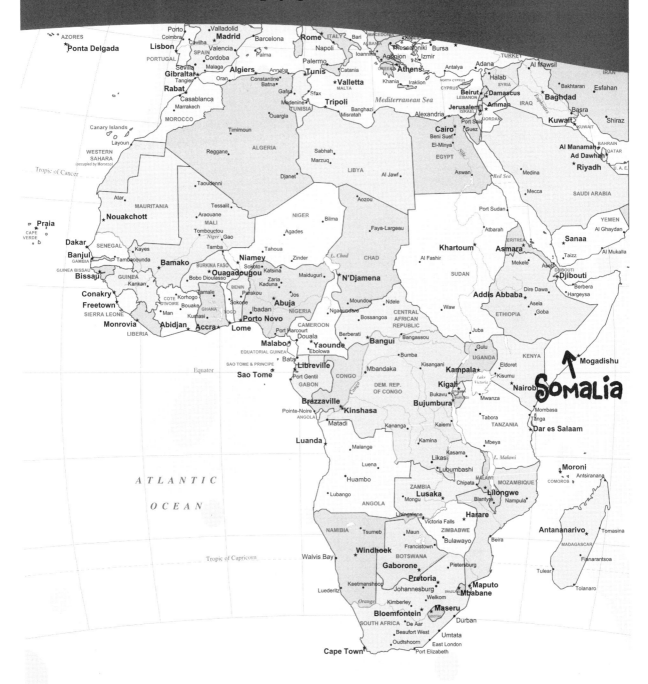

The Alpha and the Omega

Revelation 1:8 "I am the Alpha and the Omega," says the Lord God, "who is, and who was, and who is to come, the Almighty."

Date	Daily Journal

Daily Journal

Date	Daily Journal

Prayer Priorities

I want to Remember in Prayer:

_____
_____
_____
_____

Date	Daily Journal

Daily Journal

Date	Daily Journal

Alive with Christ

Ephesians 2:4-5 But because of his great love for us, God, who is rich in mercy, made us alive with Christ even when we were dead in transgressions—it is by grace you have been saved.

Date	Daily Journal

Daily Journal

Date	Daily Journal

Prayer Priorities

I want to Remember
in Prayer:

_____
_____
_____
_____

Date	Daily Journal

Daily Journal

Date	Daily Journal

Created to do good works

Ephesians 2:10 For we are God's workmanship, created in Christ Jesus to do good works, which God prepared in advance for us to do.

Date	Daily Journal

Daily Journal

Date	Daily Journal

Prayer Priorities

I want to Remember in Prayer:

_____
_____
_____
_____

Date	Daily Journal

Daily Journal

Date	Daily Journal

Daily Journal

Date	Daily Journal

Walking with God Today

MONTH: YEAR:

SUN	MON	tue	wed	thu	fri	Sat
☐	☐	☐	☐	☐	☐	☐
☐	☐	☐	☐	☐	☐	☐
☐	☐	☐	☐	☐	☐	☐
☐	☐	☐	☐	☐	☐	☐
☐	☐	☐	☐	☐	☐	☐
☐	☐	☐	☐	☐	☐	☐

Praying for Ukraine

Ukraine is one of the largest countries in Europe. Gaining independence was a long struggle for the Ukrainians, but Ukraine finally became its own country in 1991 when the Soviet Union ceased to exist. Taras Shevchenko, a national hero who wrote poetry about his love for Ukraine and his dream for freedom for his country, wrote: "Love your Ukraine, love her...in the harshest time, in the very last harsh minute pray to God for her."

Before gaining their independence, Ukrainians were discouraged from practicing any religion, and beautiful church buildings were turned into museums. Ukrainian church buildings are constructed in the shape of a cross and often have separate bell towers. Today many of these buildings are being restored and are again being used by churches.

Children are taught to be well behaved and to respect and obey their teachers. Because they are not allowed to question the authority of adults, children seldom have discipline problems in school. Elementary, middle, and high schools are not separated. All students from first through eleventh grade study together in one building.

Ukrainians love soccer and have played it for about two hundred years. Ukraine has hundreds of soccer clubs, and Ukrainian soccer players are considered among the best in the world, playing in and winning international competitions.

Ukrainians are known for making beautiful, hand-painted Easter eggs. The tradition of painting Easter eggs began as a way to celebrate the arrival of springtime and new life. Many of the painted eggs are displayed in museums for everyone to enjoy. At Easter people buy Easter eggs, have them blessed at church, and give them to family and friends as a wish for good health and a sign of friendship.

Population: 47.43 million   **Capital**: Kiev (Kyiv)   **Languages**: Ukrainian, Russian
Religion: Christian 88% Nonreligious 10% Other 2%   **Average Annual Income Per Person**: $1,040

Pray:

- for unity among all Christians in Ukraine, without competition or mistrust.
- for more teachers in Bible schools and for the availability of Christian resource and study materials.

Europe

PRESS ON toward the goal

Philippians 3:14 I press on toward the goal to win the prize for which God has called me heavenward in Christ Jesus.

Date	Daily Journal

Daily Journal

Date	Daily Journal

Prayer Priorities

I want to Remember in prayer:

_____
_____
_____
_____

Date	Daily Journal

Daily Journal

Date	Daily Journal

GOD is faithful

1 Thessalonians 5:24 The one who calls you is faithful and he will do it.

Date	Daily Journal

Daily Journal

Date	Daily Journal

Prayer Priorities

I want to Remember
in Prayer:

_____
_____
_____
_____

Date	Daily Journal

Daily Journal

Date	Daily Journal

The Lord of Peace

2 Thessalonians 3:16 Now may the Lord of peace himself give you peace at all times and in every way. The Lord be with all of you.

Date	Daily Journal

Daily Journal

Date	Daily Journal

Prayer Priorities

I want to Remember
in Prayer:
_____
_____
_____
_____

Date	Daily Journal

Daily Journal

Date	Daily Journal

Daily Journal

Date	Daily Journal

Walking with God Today

MONTH: year:

SUN	MON	tue	wed	tHu	fRi	Sat
☐	☐	☐	☐	☐	☐	☐
☐	☐	☐	☐	☐	☐	☐
☐	☐	☐	☐	☐	☐	☐
☐	☐	☐	☐	☐	☐	☐
☐	☐	☐	☐	☐	☐	☐
☐	☐	☐	☐	☐	☐	☐

Praying for the Philippines

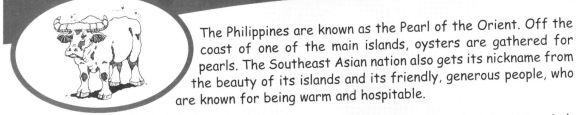

The Philippines are known as the Pearl of the Orient. Off the coast of one of the main islands, oysters are gathered for pearls. The Southeast Asian nation also gets its nickname from the beauty of its islands and its friendly, generous people, who are known for being warm and hospitable.

Christianity is very important to Filipinos. During Holy Week, the best-loved religious holiday in the Philippines, many people construct shrines containing the crucifix (a figure of Jesus on the cross). In most villages a drama showing scenes of Christ's life is staged every night of Holy Week. On Good Friday, men often carry crosses through the streets. Easter Sunday is a joyous day when children jump as high as they can as a symbol of the risen Christ. It is traditionally believed that this will make the children grow tall.

In the mountain regions of the Philippines, many people grow rice on terraces built into the side of the mountains. Some have called these impressive terraces the Eighth Wonder of the World. In some places, carabaos (water buffaloes) are still used to plow the rice paddies, although tractors have replaced many of them. Children enjoy riding the carabaos.

The capital city, Manila, is home to ten million people—three million of whom live in shanty-towns, poor areas consisting of many shacks. Other areas in Manila are home to very wealthy people.

Jeepneys are a common sight in towns and cities all over the Philippines. Jeepneys are old U.S. army jeeps often decorated with curtains, posters, lights, bright colors, horses, and statues of Jesus or Mary. Usually loaded with people, jeepneys quickly weave in and out of slower traffic. The jeepney is the fastest, cheapest, and most popular way to travel.

Population: 87.86 million **Capital:** Manila **Languages:** Filipino (based on Tagalog), English, tribal languages **Religion:** Christian 90% Muslim 8% Nonreligious/Animist 2%
Average Annual Income Per Person: $1,200

Pray:

- for more churches and people to work among the poor.
- for the Christians to have a hunger to know God.

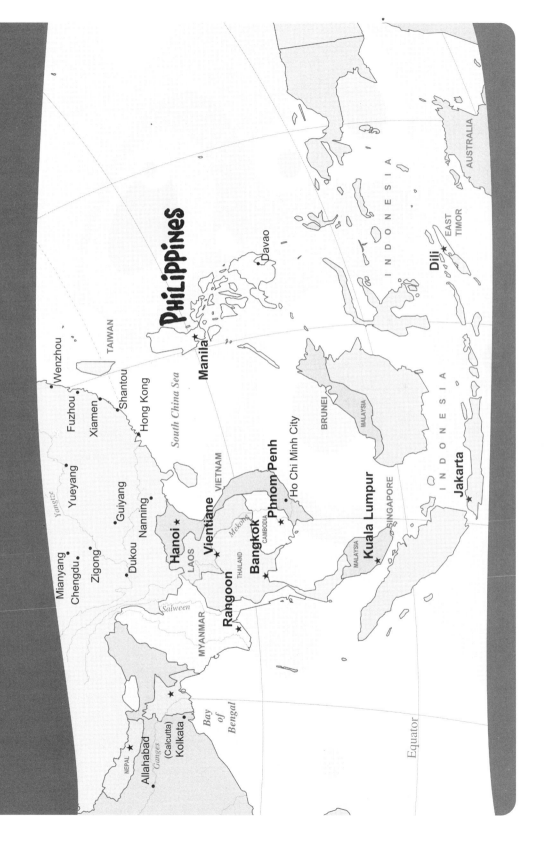

Southeast Asia

Forever the Same

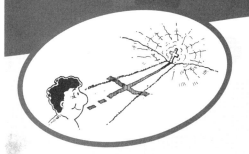

Hebrews 13:8 Jesus Christ is the same yesterday and today and forever.

Date	Daily Journal

Daily Journal

Date	Daily Journal

Prayer Priorities

I want to Remember in Prayer:

_____

_____

_____

_____

Date	Daily Journal

Daily Journal

Date	Daily Journal

Every good gift

James 1:17 Every good and perfect gift is from above, coming down from the Father of the heavenly lights, who does not change like shifting shadows.

Date	Daily Journal

Daily Journal

Date	Daily Journal

Prayer Priorities

I want to Remember
in Prayer:

_____
_____
_____
_____

Date	Daily Journal

Daily Journal

Date	Daily Journal

Walk in the Light

1 JOHN 1:7 But if we walk in the light, as he is in the light, we have fellowship with one another, and the blood of Jesus, his Son, purifies us from all sin.

Date	Daily Journal

Daily Journal

Date	Daily Journal

Prayer Priorities

I want to Remember
in Prayer:

Date	Daily Journal

Daily Journal

Date	Daily Journal

Daily Journal

Date	Daily Journal

Walking with God Today

MONTH: _____   year: _____

SUN	MON	tue	wed	tHu	fri	sat

Praying for Nicaragua

Nicaragua is located in the middle of Central America. The Nicaraguan forest is home to interesting animals such as sloths, anteaters, armadillos, monkeys, alligators, and snakes. Earthquakes, volcanoes, and hurricanes are common in this country. The capital city, Managua, has been flattened twice by earthquakes (1931 and 1972).

Nicaragua is an important coffee grower for the world, and harvesting the coffee produces jobs for many men, women, and children. Because Nicaragua relies on its coffee crops, it is disastrous when a hurricane or flood wipes out entire crops within hours. Only about half the people who are able to work can find a job. Many try to survive by selling items such as buckets, shoes, sweets, and snacks on the street.

Although many Nicaraguans are poor, if a neighbor stops by to chat while a person is cooking and "helps" by stirring the pot or throwing in a few spices, the neighbor is given a serving when the meal is ready. Since Nicaraguans believe that they will have bad luck if others see them being stingy, it is their custom to share with everyone who sees them preparing or even hears that they are preparing a special meal.

Family life is important to Nicaraguans. The average family has six children, and a household usually includes cousins, aunts, uncles, and grandparents. A favorite pastime is to sit on a front porch and talk, tell stories, or listen to the radio. Baseball is Nicaragua's national sport. Children grow up playing baseball on the streets and in fields, parks, and vacant lots. If they don't have a bat or a baseball, they will use a stick and a handmade ball.

Population: 5.47 million   **Capital:** Managua   **Languages:** Spanish, English, Miskito
Religion: Christian 90% Nonreligious/other 10%   **Average Annual Income Per**
Person: $410

Pray:

- for unity among Christians. The church in Nicaragua has been growing rapidly, and if the Christians work together, they can help their country.
- that the church will find practical ways to help those with no jobs or homes.

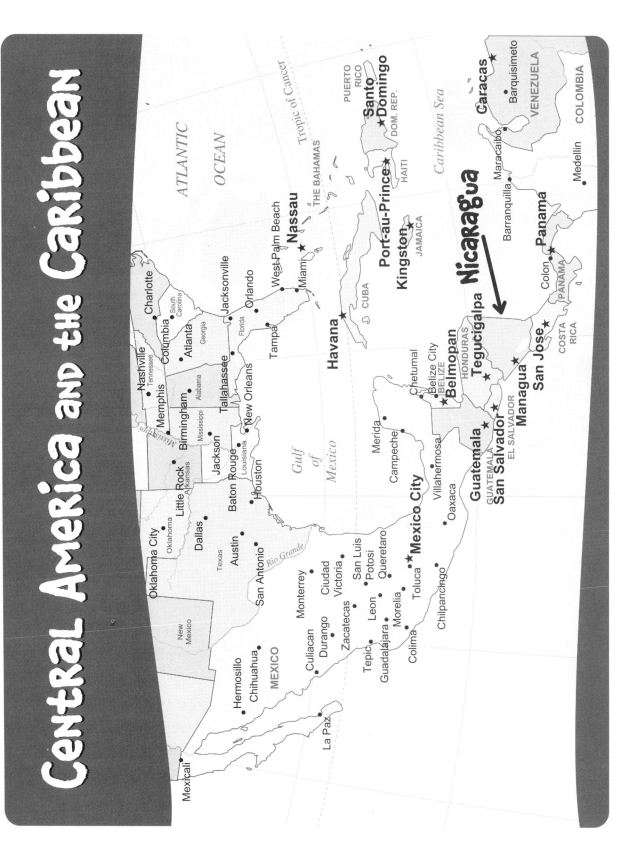

Exalt the LORD

PSALM 99:5 Exalt the LORD our God and worship at his footstool; he is holy.

Date	Daily Journal

Daily Journal

Date	Daily Journal

Prayer Priorities

I want to Remember in Prayer:

_____

_____

_____

_____

Date	Daily Journal

Daily Journal

Date	Daily Journal

Be merciful

Luke 6:36 "Be merciful, just as your Father is merciful."

Date	Daily Journal

Daily Journal

Date	Daily Journal

Prayer Priorities

I want to Remember
in Prayer:

_____
_____
_____
_____

Date	Daily Journal

Daily Journal

Date	Daily Journal

God is able

2 Corinthians 9:8 And God is able to make all grace abound to you, so that in all things at all times, having all that you need, you will abound in every good work.

Date	Daily Journal

Daily Journal

Date	Daily Journal

Prayer Priorities

I want to Remember in Prayer: _____
_____
_____
_____

Date	Daily Journal

Daily Journal

Date	Daily Journal

Daily Journal

Date	Daily Journal

Walking with God Today

MONTH: **YEAR:**

SUN	MON	tue	wed	thu	fri	Sat

Praying for Senegal

Senegal is one of Africa's smallest countries. Yet the capital city, Dakar, is one of the most important seaports on the coast of West Africa. It can handle forty to fifty oceangoing vessels at one time. Dakar is also one of Africa's most modern cities, with elegant streets and office buildings.

The small island of Goree, off the coast of Senegal, is known as the Island of Sorrows. In the late 1550s Goree became a major center for the slave trade. Today, however, Goree is a tourist center for sunbathing, swimming, and picnicking.

Senegal's inland is home to elephants, lions, antelopes, panthers, cheetahs, and jackals. In the marshes, warthogs are common. Living in the forests along the rivers are many kinds of monkeys and such dangerous snakes as pythons, boa constrictors, vipers, cobras, and mambas.

The largest people group in Senegal, the Wolof, are mostly farmers. They plant their fields in rings around their villages so that they can easily tend to their crops. The inner-most ring contains the vegetable gardens in which the women and children work.

Most Wolof villages have a mosque (a Muslim place of worship), a public gathering place with plenty of shade, and a well or other source of water. Each village's religious life is directed by a *marabout*, a wise man who can read and write Arabic and knows the Koran (the Muslim holy book).

Only about half of Wolof families can afford to send their children to school because the children are needed to work in the fields. Almost all schools in Senegal teach in French, the official language, but most Senegalese children speak Wolof and other tribal languages, not French. As a result, only 33 percent of Senegal's people are able to read and write.

Population: 11.13 million   **Capital:** Dakar   **Languages:** French, Wolof and other tribal languages   **Religion:** Muslim 94% Christian 5% Traditional religions 1%   **Average Annual Income Per Person:** $3,410

Pray:

- for the Muslims of Senegal, who remain almost totally unreached by the gospel.
- for the young people who are flocking to the city and are more open to hearing the gospel.

Africa

Senegal

Do Not turn aside

Deuteronomy 5:32 So be careful to do what the LORD your God has commanded you; do not turn aside to the right or to the left.

Date	Daily Journal

Daily Journal

Date	Daily Journal

Prayer Priorities

I want to Remember
in Prayer:

_____
_____
_____
_____

Date	Daily Journal

Daily Journal

Date	Daily Journal

How majestic is your name

Psalm 8:1 O LORD, our Lord, how majestic is your name in all the earth! You have set your glory above the heavens.

Date	Daily Journal

Daily Journal

Date	Daily Journal

Prayer Priorities

I want to Remember
in Prayer:

_____
_____
_____
_____

Date	Daily Journal

Daily Journal

Date	Daily Journal

THe KiNG oF gLoRY

PsaLM 24:8 Who is this King of glory? The LORD strong and mighty, the LORD mighty in battle.

Date	Daily JouRNal

Daily Journal

Date	Daily Journal

Prayer Priorities

I want to Remember
in Prayer:
_____
_____
_____
_____

Date	Daily Journal

Daily Journal

Date	Daily Journal

Daily Journal

Date	Daily Journal

WALKING with GOD Today

MONTH: _____   YEAR: _____

SUN	MON	TUE	WED	THU	FRI	SAT
☐	☐	☐	☐	☐	☐	☐
☐	☐	☐	☐	☐	☐	☐
☐	☐	☐	☐	☐	☐	☐
☐	☐	☐	☐	☐	☐	☐
☐	☐	☐	☐	☐	☐	☐
☐	☐	☐	☐	☐	☐	☐

Praying for Switzerland

The charming country of Switzerland is a land of watchmaking, downhill skiing, fine chocolate, and yodeling. The Swiss people are hardworking and full of adventure. They are thinkers and tinkerers who have invented cellophane, rack railways, and rollers for grinding grain. Watchmaking is a perfect job for the Swiss because it requires careful and exact work. The Swiss make more than twenty-five million watches each year, and Switzerland earns more money exporting watches than any other nation.

Every year, children's festivals and parades are held throughout Switzerland to celebrate the end of spring and the beginning of summer. The Swiss' love of young people can be seen in the classic Swiss story *Heidi*, written in 1880. Heidi is an orphan who goes to live with her loving grandfather in a village high up in the mountains. Switzerland is well known for its snowcapped mountains called the Alps. The Alps are the largest mountain range in Europe, with more than one thousand glaciers at work carving out deep valleys. Millions of tourists come to Switzerland each year to hike, swim, sail, or simply relax. Tourists have been coming to Switzerland since the late 1700s.

One of Switzerland's most famous food dishes is fondue. Fondue lovers take bits of bread, meat, or cake and dip them into melted cheese, hot oils, chocolate, or other sauces. The Swiss are known around the world for their chocolate. Chocolate factories make hundreds of varieties of chocolate in all shapes and sizes.

Switzerland is a wealthy country and has a long tradition of offering help and disaster relief to the rest of the world.

Population: 7.49 million   **Capital:** Bern   **Languages:** German, French, Italian
Religion: Christian 80% (practicing Christian closer to 40%) Nonreligious 11%
Other/unspecified 5% Muslim 4%   **Average Annual Income Per Person:** $43,060

Pray:

- that wealth and comfort will not stand in the way of the Swiss making a commitment to Jesus.
- that many people will be called into full-time Christian work.

Europe

My Soul Pants for you

Psalm 42:1 As the deer pants for streams of water, so my soul pants for you, O God.

Date	Daily Journal

Daily Journal

Date	Daily Journal

Prayer Priorities

I want to Remember
in Prayer:
_____
_____
_____
_____

Date	Daily Journal

Daily Journal

Date	Daily Journal

Be Still

Psalm 46:10 "Be still, and know that I am God; I will be exalted among the nations, I will be exalted in the earth."

Date	Daily Journal

Daily Journal

Date	Daily Journal

Prayer Priorities

I want to Remember
in Prayer:
_____
_____
_____
_____

Date	Daily Journal

Daily Journal

Date	Daily Journal

Do not Say...

Jeremiah 1:7 But the LORD said to me, "Do not say, 'I am only a child.' You must go to everyone I send you to and say whatever I command you."

Date	Daily Journal

Daily Journal

Date	Daily Journal

Prayer Priorities

I want to Remember
in Prayer:

_____
_____
_____
_____

Date	Daily Journal

Daily Journal

Date	Daily Journal

Daily Journal

Date	Daily Journal

Walking with God Today

MONTH: _____   YEAR: _____

Sun	Mon	tue	wed	tHu	fri	Sat
☐	☐	☐	☐	☐	☐	☐
☐	☐	☐	☐	☐	☐	☐
☐	☐	☐	☐	☐	☐	☐
☐	☐	☐	☐	☐	☐	☐
☐	☐	☐	☐	☐	☐	☐
☐	☐	☐	☐	☐	☐	☐

Praying for the Cuna

Off the eastern shore of Panama, in the Caribbean Sea, is a small group of islands called the San Blas Islands. The majority of the Cuna Indians live on these islands. A small group of Cuna live on the Panama mainland, in the Darien Gap, a dense jungle with swarms of mosquitoes and wild animals.

Cuna adults are relatively short. If a Cuna man or woman is 5 feet 2 inches (1.58 meters) tall, he or she is considered very tall. Cuna women traditionally wear gold rings in both the nose and the ears. Mothers pierce their baby girls' noses when the babies are only one month old.

The Cuna live in thatched-palm huts with bamboo walls. Family ties are very important to the Cuna, and many members of one family will live in a single hut. Cuna men typically farm, hunt, and fish, while Cuna women tend to the home and take care of the children. Women usually do not leave the settlement, but men will often leave for years and go to college.

Cuna women make beautiful, intricately stitched cloths called *molas*. Molas have geometric designs or pictures of animals, birds, or village scenes. A mola may require eighty hours of labor. Cuna women have been making molas for hundreds of years, and molas are a source of income for the Cunas.

To achieve honor in the next life, after death, the Cunas believe that they must achieve a high level of honor in this life. One way to achieve honor is to collect the teeth of the white-faced monkey, a fierce animal. The Cunas hunt the monkey and put its teeth on a necklace. The more monkeys a Cuna kills, the more the Cuna will be rewarded in the next life.

Missionaries have worked among the Cuna people, mostly in the San Blas Islands, yet many Cunas mix their traditional beliefs and practices with Christianity. A missionary is currently translating the Bible into Cuna, a slow and challenging task. Until recently, the Cuna language was spoken but never written.

Population: 61,700 **Languages:** Cuna, Spanish **Religion:** Christian 85% (often mixed with the Cunas' traditional ethnic religion) **Average Annual Income Per Person in Panama:** $7,600

Pray:

- for the gospel to be preached in the Darien Gap. Because of violence and the dense jungle, Darien Province is virtually closed to missionaries.
- for the completion of a Bible translation in the Cuna language.

Central America and the Caribbean

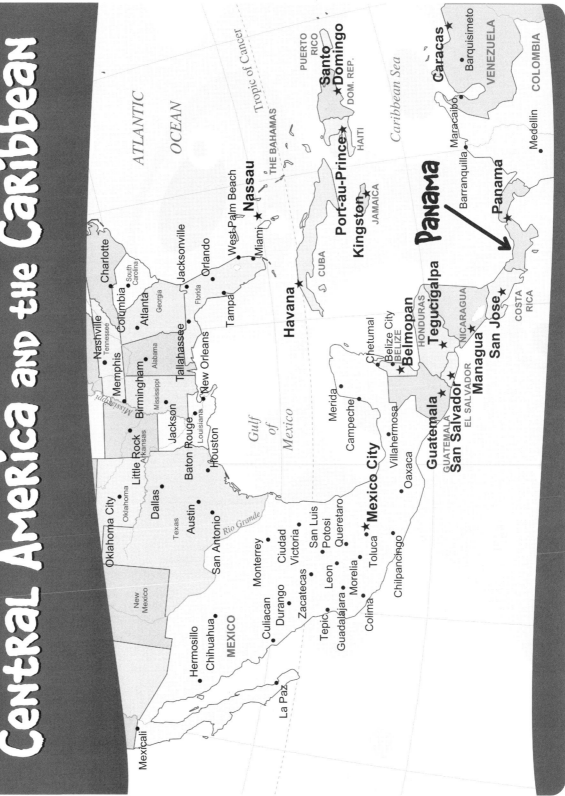

An everlasting love

Jeremiah 31:3 The LORD appeared to us in the past, saying: "I have loved you with an everlasting love; I have drawn you with loving-kindness."

Date	Daily Journal

Daily Journal

Date	Daily Journal

Prayer Priorities

I want to Remember
in Prayer:

_____

_____

_____

_____

Date	Daily Journal

Daily Journal

Date	Daily Journal

He who has the Son...

1 JOHN 5:12 He who has the Son has life; he who does not have the Son of God does not have life.

Date	Daily Journal

Daily Journal

Date	Daily Journal

Prayer Priorities

I want to Remember
in Prayer:

Date	Daily Journal

Daily Journal

Date	Daily Journal

Set an example

1 Timothy 4:12 Don't let anyone look down on you because you are young, but set an example for the believers in speech, in life, in love, in faith and in purity.

Date	Daily Journal

Daily Journal

Date	Daily Journal

Prayer Priorities

I want to Remember
in Prayer:

_____
_____
_____
_____

Date	Daily Journal

Daily Journal

Date	Daily Journal

Daily Journal

Date	Daily Journal

Walking with God Today

MONTH: **year:**

SuN	MON	tue	weD	tHu	fRi	sat
☐	☐	☐	☐	☐	☐	☐
☐	☐	☐	☐	☐	☐	☐
☐	☐	☐	☐	☐	☐	☐
☐	☐	☐	☐	☐	☐	☐
☐	☐	☐	☐	☐	☐	☐
☐	☐	☐	☐	☐	☐	☐

Praying for Malaysia

Malaysia consists of West Malaysia, on the Malay Peninsula, and East Malaysia, on the island of Borneo. The two sections are divided by four hundred miles of the South China Sea. Malaysia has two seasons—wet and very wet. Monsoons (seasonal winds that blow across the ocean and deposit heavy rain) occur in Malaysia nearly all year long. As a result, much of Malaysia is covered by tropical forests.

A variety of animals live in Malaysia's jungles, including a rare orangutan. Various types of monkeys are also a common sight, even near cities. Large crocodiles are common in Malaysia's rivers, and the country is home to more than one hundred species of snakes.

Three large ethnic groups make up Malaysia: the Malays, the Chinese, and the Indians. The Malays are mainly farmers and fishermen who live near rivers or streams. Chinese Malaysians are often shopkeepers and business people. Most Indians in Malaysia came from the southeastern Indian state of Tamil Nadu and were first brought to Malaysia to do manual labor. Today the Indians make up a large part of the workforce on the Malaysian railway system.

Although freedom of religion is guaranteed by law in Malaysia, Islam is the country's official religion. At five or six, a Malay boy is sent to a teacher to learn Muslim scriptures. Girls also must learn the art of reading the scriptures. The Koran is the most important holy book of Islam, and reading the entire Koran usually takes about five years. In Islamic tradition, at the end of a holy month, Malay boys and girls kiss their parents' hands and beg for forgiveness.

A Malaysian sport called *sepak takraw* (Malaysian football) combines features of volleyball and soccer. The players may not touch the ball with their hands or arms. They use their feet or heads to knock the lightweight ball across a net.

Population: 23.95 million   **Capital:** Kuala Lumpur   **Languages:** Bahasa Malayu, English, Chinese, Indian languages   **Religion:** Muslim 56% Buddhist 20% Hindu 13% Christian 9% Other 2%   **Average Annual Income Per Person:** $4,530

Pray:

- for true freedom of religion. Worship services in private homes are discouraged.
- for missionaries to be able to reach those who haven't heard the gospel yet. Pray also for more missionaries to get visas, which are difficult to obtain.

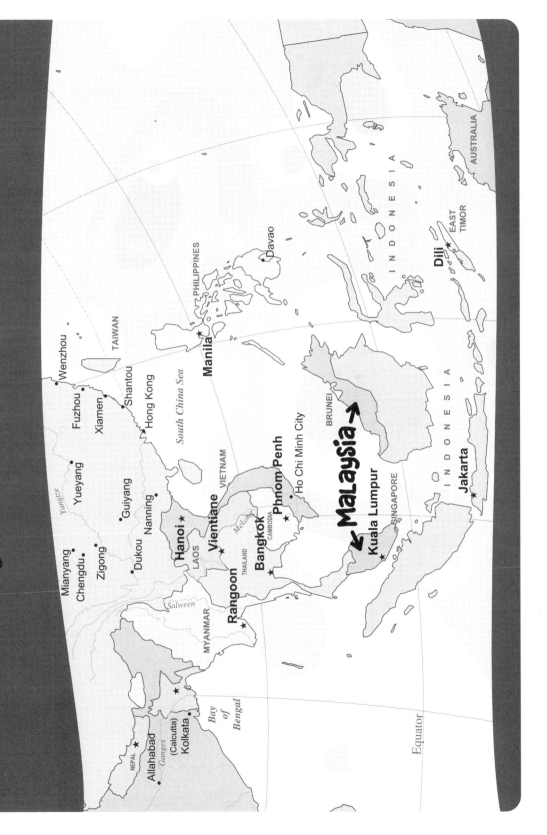

No greater joy

3 JOHN 4 I have no greater joy than to hear that my children are walking in the truth.

Date	Daily Journal

Daily Journal

Date	Daily Journal

Prayer Priorities

I want to Remember
in Prayer:

_____

_____

_____

_____

Date	Daily Journal

Daily Journal

Date	Daily Journal

WHOM SHALL I FEAR?

PSALM 27:1 The LORD is my light and my salvation—whom shall I fear? The LORD is the stronghold of my life—of whom shall I be afraid?

Date	Daily Journal

Daily Journal

Date	Daily Journal

Prayer Priorities

I want to Remember in Prayer:

_____
_____
_____
_____

Date	Daily Journal

Daily Journal

Date	Daily Journal

Abounding in Love

Psalm 86:15 But you, O Lord, are a compassionate and gracious God, slow to anger, abounding in love and faithfulness.

Date	Daily Journal

Daily Journal

Date	Daily Journal

Prayer Priorities

I want to Remember in Prayer:

Date	Daily Journal

Daily Journal

Date	Daily Journal

Daily Journal

Date	Daily Journal

Walking with God Today

month: **year:**

Sun	Mon	tue	wed	thu	fri	Sat

Praying for Pakistan

The country of Pakistan was born because of a need for Muslims in India to have a country of their own. Because of this, Pakistan is almost entirely a Muslim nation. Five times a day, religious Muslims will stop to say their prayers, no matter where they might be. Before praying, they must wash their faces and hands and make sure their bodies and clothes are clean.

One of the most important duties of the family is to teach religion to the children. Pakistani families are usually large because children are considered a gift. Great-grandparents, grandparents, parents, and children often live in the same house together. Respect is always given to the oldest members of the family. Children are taught to obey their fathers, and they are expected to continue to obey them even when they themselves are grown up and have children of their own.

Marriages are usually arranged in advance by the parents, often before the children have been born. Sometimes the bride and groom will meet for the very first time on their wedding day. Dating is not allowed in Pakistan.

Children in poor families often help out with the family business of farming, fishing, carpentry, or carpet weaving. Because of their small hands and fingers, children are able to make especially beautiful carpets. Sadly, some carpet factories make children work twelve-hour days and pay them hardly anything. Children in most wealthier families do not work. They instead go to school, study, and play. Kite flying is a favorite activity, and children often make their own kites from plastic bags and sticks. Some boys glue broken glass to their kite strings and have kite fights in the sky.

Pakistanis dress modestly. Both men and women wear loose-fitting, pajama-like trousers called *shalwar*. Most women cover their heads with a scarf or shawl. Men wear turbans wrapped around their heads.

Population: 164.42 million **Capital:** Islamabad **Languages:** Urdu, English, Punjabi, Sindhi, Pashtu, Balochi, Brahvi, Siraiki **Religion:** Muslim 97% Christian/Hindu/ other 3% **Average Annual Income Per Person:** $500

Pray:

- for Christians who are killed or imprisoned for their faith—that they will receive strength and courage from God.
- that the New Testament will be translated into the thirty-eight language groups that do not yet have it.

Asia

Pakistan

He will not fall

Psalm 37:23-24 If the LORD delights in a man's way, he makes his steps firm; though he stumble, he will not fall, for the LORD upholds him with his hand.

Date	Daily Journal

Daily Journal

Date	Daily Journal

Prayer Priorities

I want to Remember
in prayer:

_____

_____

_____

_____

Date	Daily Journal

Daily Journal

Date	Daily Journal

Great things

PSALM 126:2 Our mouths were filled with laughter, our tongues with songs of joy. Then it was said among the nations, "The LORD has done great things for them."

Date	Daily Journal

Daily Journal

Date	Daily Journal

Prayer Priorities

I want to Remember
in Prayer:

_____
_____
_____
_____

Date	Daily Journal

Daily Journal

Date	Daily Journal

He Hears us

1 JOHN 5:14 This is the confidence we have in approaching God: that if we ask anything according to his will, he hears us.

Date	Daily Journal

Daily Journal

Date	Daily Journal

Prayer Priorities

I want to Remember in Prayer:

_____
_____
_____
_____

Date	Daily Journal

Daily Journal

Date	Daily Journal

Daily Journal

Date	Daily Journal

Walking with God Today

MONTH: **YEAR:**

SUN	MON	tue	wed	tHu	fri	Sat
☐	☐	☐	☐	☐	☐	☐
☐	☐	☐	☐	☐	☐	☐
☐	☐	☐	☐	☐	☐	☐
☐	☐	☐	☐	☐	☐	☐
☐	☐	☐	☐	☐	☐	☐
☐	☐	☐	☐	☐	☐	☐

Praying for Trinidad & Tobago

Trinidad and Tobago is a country made up of two small islands in the Caribbean Sea, off the northeastern coast of Venezuela. Some historians believe that these were the first islands in the Caribbean to be occupied by humans. Throughout history, numerous nations settled on these islands, and the people are a mix of Carib Indian, French Creole, Spanish, English, Portuguese, Italian, Chinese, Indian, Lebanese, and, most numerous, the descendants of African slaves. Trinidad, the larger of the two islands, is busy, noisy, and polluted. In Tobago, life is slow and easygoing, and tiny villages dot the countryside.

The land and water of Trinidad and Tobago are home to crocodiles, many kinds of birds, iguanas, manatees, and five species of turtles. The largest turtle is the leatherback, which can grow to seven feet and weigh twelve hundred pounds. Leatherbacks can be seen on land when they come ashore to bury their eggs in the sand.

Coconut juice is sold almost everywhere by street vendors, who use machetes to split open the coconuts. Experienced vendors can tell whether a coconut is ripe and ready to be opened simply by shaking it.

The steel drum, also called the "pan," originated on Trinidad and is extremely popular. Calypso music is a way of life on the islands, and radio is more popular than television. The people of Trinidad and Tobago enjoy leisure time. Hanging out, or "liming," is very popular. Liming has no structure to it. A good limer has lots of time and knows how to appreciate doing nothing. A typical lime might be talking with friends outside of a department store, in the park, or in someone's yard.

Cricket is the national pastime in Trinidad and Tobago. Most parks have several cricket pitches (fields), and children often set up cricket matches on the street. When children are not playing or watching cricket matches, they can often be found playing soccer.

Population: 1.01 million   **Capital:** Port of Spain   **Languages:** English (official language), Hindi, French, Spanish, Chinese   **Religion:** Christian 58% Hindu 22% Other/non-religious 14% Muslim 6%   **Average Annual Income Per Person:** $4,250

Pray:

- that the churches on both islands will unite with common goals to reach their country and other surrounding countries.
- for the youth ministries working in the schools to reach students with the gospel.

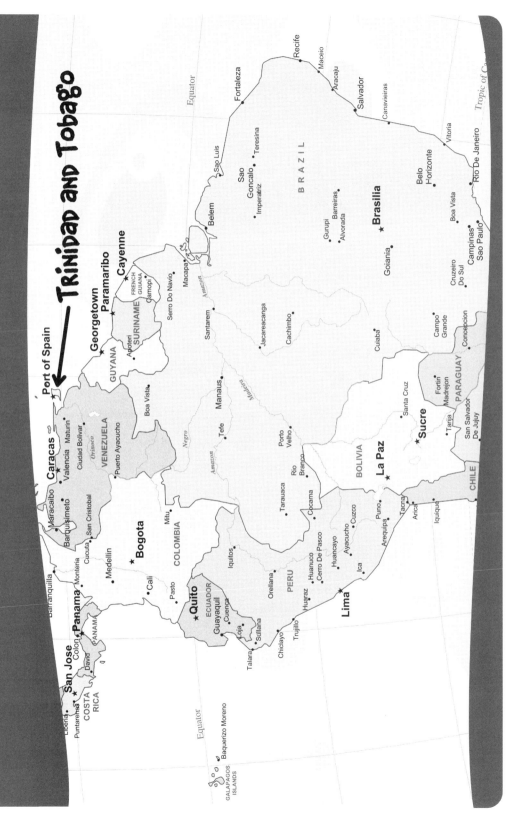

South America

Trinidad and Tobago

Port of Spain

Equator

Tropic of C...

GALAPAGOS ISLANDS

Equator

Baquerizo Moreno

COSTA RICA
★ San Jose
Liberia
Puntarenas
Colon ★ Panama
David
PANAMA

Barranquilla

Maracaibo
Barquisimeto
Valencia ★ Caracas
Maturin
San Cristobal
Ciudad Bolivar
VENEZUELA
Orinoco
Puerto Ayacucho

Cucuta
Monteria
Medellin
Cali
Pasto
★ Bogota
COLOMBIA
Mitu

Boa Vista

Georgetown
Paramaribo ★ Cayenne
GUYANA
SURINAME
FRENCH GUIANA
Apoteri
Gamopi
Serro Do Navio

Macapa
Amazon

★ Quito
ECUADOR
Guayaquil
Cuenca
Loja
Talara
Sullana
Chiclayo
Trujillo

Orellana
Iquitos

Belem

Santarem

Manaus

Tefe

Negro

Jacareacanga
Cachimbo

São Luis
Fortaleza

São Goncalo
Teresina
Imperatriz

Recife
Maceio
Aracaju
Salvador
Canavieiras

PERU
Huaraz
Cerro De Pasco
Huanuco
Huancayo
★ Lima
Ica
Ayacucho
Cuzco
Arequipa
Puno
Tacna
Arica
Iquique

Tarauaca
Cocama
Rio Branco
Porto Velho
Madeira
Amazon

Cuiaba

Campo Grande

Gurupi
Barreiras
Alvorada
★ Brasilia
Goiania
Cruzeiro Do Sul
Belo Horizonte
Boa Vista
Campinas
São Paulo
Vitoria
Rio De Janeiro

B R A Z I L

Santa Cruz
BOLIVIA
★ La Paz
★ Sucre
Fortin Madrejon
PARAGUAY
Concepcion
Tarija
San Salvador De Jujuy

CHILE

Not by might

Zechariah 4:6 "Not by might nor by power, but by my Spirit," says the LORD Almighty.

Date	Daily Journal

Daily Journal

Date	Daily Journal

Prayer Priorities

I want to Remember
in Prayer:
_____
_____
_____
_____

Date	Daily Journal

Daily Journal

Date	Daily Journal

THE LORD IS MY STRENGTH

Habakkuk 3:19 The Sovereign LORD is my strength; he makes my feet like the feet of a deer, he enables me to go on the heights.

Date	Daily Journal

Daily Journal

Date	Daily Journal

Prayer Priorities

I want to Remember in Prayer:

_____
_____
_____
_____

Date	Daily Journal

Daily Journal

Date	Daily Journal

Great is your faithfulness

Lamentations 3:22-23 Because of the LORD's great love we are not consumed, for his compassions never fail. They are new every morning; great is your faithfulness.

Date	Daily Journal

Daily Journal

Date	Daily Journal

Prayer Priorities

I want to Remember in Prayer:

_____
_____
_____
_____

Date	Daily Journal

Daily Journal

Date	Daily Journal

Unfailing Love

Isaiah 54:10 "Though the mountains be shaken and the hills be removed, yet my unfailing love for you will not be shaken nor my covenant of peace be removed," says the LORD, who has compassion on you.

Date	Daily Journal

Daily Journal

Date	Daily Journal

Bible Reading Plan: Track 1

- ❏ Matthew 1, 2
- ❏ Matthew 3
- ❏ Matthew 4
- ❏ Matthew 5
- ❏ Matthew 6, 7
- ❏ Matthew 8
- ❏ Matthew 9
- ❏ Matthew 10
- ❏ Matthew 11
- ❏ Matthew 12
- ❏ Matthew 13
- ❏ Matthew 14
- ❏ Matthew 15
- ❏ Matthew 16
- ❏ Matthew 17
- ❏ Matthew 18
- ❏ Matthew 19
- ❏ Matthew 20
- ❏ Matthew 21
- ❏ Matthew 22
- ❏ Matthew 23
- ❏ Matthew 24
- ❏ Matthew 25
- ❏ Matthew 26
- ❏ Matthew 27
- ❏ Matthew 28
- ❏ Mark 1
- ❏ Mark 2
- ❏ Mark 3
- ❏ Mark 4
- ❏ Mark 5
- ❏ Mark 6
- ❏ Mark 7
- ❏ Mark 8
- ❏ Mark 9
- ❏ Mark 10
- ❏ Mark 11
- ❏ Mark 12
- ❏ Mark 13
- ❏ Mark 14
- ❏ Mark 15
- ❏ Mark 16

- ❏ Luke 1
- ❏ Luke 2
- ❏ Luke 3
- ❏ Luke 4
- ❏ Luke 5
- ❏ Luke 6
- ❏ Luke 7
- ❏ Luke 8
- ❏ Luke 9
- ❏ Luke 10
- ❏ Luke 11
- ❏ Luke 12
- ❏ Luke 13
- ❏ Luke 14
- ❏ Luke 15
- ❏ Luke 16
- ❏ Luke 17
- ❏ Luke 18
- ❏ Luke 19
- ❏ Luke 20
- ❏ Luke 21
- ❏ Luke 22
- ❏ Luke 23
- ❏ Luke 24
- ❏ John 1
- ❏ John 2, 3
- ❏ John 4
- ❏ John 5
- ❏ John 6
- ❏ John 7
- ❏ John 8
- ❏ John 9
- ❏ John 10
- ❏ John 11
- ❏ John 12
- ❏ John 13
- ❏ John 14
- ❏ John 15
- ❏ John 16
- ❏ John 17
- ❏ John 18
- ❏ John 19

- ❏ John 20, 21
- ❏ Acts 1
- ❏ Acts 2
- ❏ Acts 3
- ❏ Acts 4, 5
- ❏ Acts 6
- ❏ Acts 7
- ❏ Acts 8
- ❏ Acts 9
- ❏ Acts 10
- ❏ Acts 11, 12
- ❏ Acts 13
- ❏ Acts 14
- ❏ Acts 15
- ❏ Acts 16
- ❏ Acts 17
- ❏ Acts 18
- ❏ Acts 19, 20
- ❏ Acts 21
- ❏ Acts 22
- ❏ Acts 23
- ❏ Acts 24, 25
- ❏ Acts 26
- ❏ Acts 27, 28
- ❏ Romans 1
- ❏ Romans 2
- ❏ Romans 3
- ❏ Romans 4
- ❏ Romans 5
- ❏ Romans 6
- ❏ Romans 7
- ❏ Romans 8
- ❏ Romans 9
- ❏ Romans 10
- ❏ Romans 11
- ❏ Romans 12
- ❏ Romans 13
- ❏ Romans 14
- ❏ Romans 15, 16
- ❏ 1 Corinthians 1
- ❏ 1 Corinthians 2, 3
- ❏ 1 Corinthians 4, 5

- ❏ 1 Corinthians 6
- ❏ 1 Corinthians 7
- ❏ 1 Corinthians 8, 9
- ❏ 1 Corinthians 10
- ❏ 1 Corinthians 11
- ❏ 1 Corinthians 12, 13
- ❏ 1 Corinthians 14
- ❏ 1 Corinthians 15
- ❏ 1 Corinthians 16
- ❏ 2 Corinthians 1
- ❏ 2 Corinthians 2, 3
- ❏ 2 Corinthians 4, 5
- ❏ 2 Corinthians 6, 7
- ❏ 2 Corinthians 8
- ❏ 2 Corinthians 9, 10
- ❏ 2 Corinthians 11
- ❏ 2 Corinthians 12
- ❏ 2 Corinthians 13
- ❏ Galatians 1
- ❏ Galatians 2
- ❏ Galatians 3
- ❏ Galatians 4
- ❏ Galatians 5
- ❏ Galatians 6
- ❏ Ephesians 1
- ❏ Ephesians 2, 3
- ❏ Ephesians 4
- ❏ Ephesians 5
- ❏ Ephesians 6
- ❏ Philippians 1
- ❏ Philippians 2
- ❏ Philippians 3, 4
- ❏ Colossians 1
- ❏ Colossians 2, 3
- ❏ Colossians 4
- ❏ 1 Thessalonians 1, 2
- ❏ 1 Thessalonians 3, 4
- ❏ 1 Thessalonians 5
- ❏ 2 Thessalonians 1, 2
- ❏ 2 Thessalonians 3
- ❏ 1 Timothy 1, 2
- ❏ 1 Timothy 3, 4

- [ ] 1 Timothy 5, 6
- [ ] 2 Timothy 1, 2
- [ ] 2 Timothy 3, 4
- [ ] Titus 1
- [ ] Titus 2, 3
- [ ] Philemon
- [ ] Hebrews 1
- [ ] Hebrews 2
- [ ] Hebrews 3, 4
- [ ] Hebrews 5
- [ ] Hebrews 6
- [ ] Hebrews 7, 8
- [ ] Hebrews 9
- [ ] Hebrews 10
- [ ] Hebrews 11
- [ ] Hebrews 12
- [ ] Hebrews 13
- [ ] James 1
- [ ] James 2
- [ ] James 3, 4
- [ ] James 5
- [ ] 1 Peter 1
- [ ] 1 Peter 2
- [ ] 1 Peter 3
- [ ] 1 Peter 4, 5
- [ ] 2 Peter 1
- [ ] 2 Peter 2
- [ ] 2 Peter 3
- [ ] 1 John 1, 2
- [ ] 1 John 3, 4
- [ ] 1 John 5
- [ ] 2 John, 3 John
- [ ] Jude
- [ ] Revelation 1
- [ ] Revelation 2
- [ ] Revelation 3
- [ ] Revelation 4, 5
- [ ] Revelation 6, 7
- [ ] Revelation 8, 9
- [ ] Revelation 10, 11
- [ ] Revelation 12, 13
- [ ] Revelation 14, 15
- [ ] Revelation 16, 17
- [ ] Revelation 18
- [ ] Revelation 19
- [ ] Revelation 20
- [ ] Revelation 21
- [ ] Revelation 22
- [ ] Psalm 1
- [ ] Psalm 2

- [ ] Psalm 3
- [ ] Psalm 4
- [ ] Psalm 5
- [ ] Psalm 6
- [ ] Psalm 7
- [ ] Psalm 8
- [ ] Psalm 9
- [ ] Psalm 10
- [ ] Psalm 11
- [ ] Psalm 12
- [ ] Psalm 13
- [ ] Psalm 14
- [ ] Psalm 15
- [ ] Psalm 16
- [ ] Psalm 17
- [ ] Psalm 18
- [ ] Psalm 19
- [ ] Psalm 20
- [ ] Psalm 21
- [ ] Psalm 22
- [ ] Psalm 23
- [ ] Psalm 24
- [ ] Psalm 25
- [ ] Psalm 26
- [ ] Psalm 27
- [ ] Psalm 28
- [ ] Psalm 29
- [ ] Psalm 30
- [ ] Psalm 31
- [ ] Psalm 32
- [ ] Psalm 33
- [ ] Psalm 34
- [ ] Psalm 35
- [ ] Psalm 36
- [ ] Psalm 37
- [ ] Psalm 38
- [ ] Psalm 39
- [ ] Psalm 40
- [ ] Psalm 41
- [ ] Psalm 42
- [ ] Psalm 43
- [ ] Psalm 44
- [ ] Psalm 45
- [ ] Psalm 46
- [ ] Psalm 47
- [ ] Psalm 48
- [ ] Psalm 49
- [ ] Psalm 50
- [ ] Psalm 51
- [ ] Psalm 52

- [ ] Psalm 53
- [ ] Psalm 54
- [ ] Psalm 55
- [ ] Psalm 56
- [ ] Psalm 57
- [ ] Psalm 58
- [ ] Psalm 59
- [ ] Psalm 60
- [ ] Psalm 61
- [ ] Psalm 62
- [ ] Psalm 63
- [ ] Psalm 64
- [ ] Psalm 65
- [ ] Psalm 66
- [ ] Psalm 67
- [ ] Psalm 68
- [ ] Psalm 69
- [ ] Psalm 70
- [ ] Psalm 71
- [ ] Psalm 72
- [ ] Psalm 73
- [ ] Psalm 74
- [ ] Psalm 75
- [ ] Psalm 76
- [ ] Psalm 77
- [ ] Psalm 78
- [ ] Psalm 79
- [ ] Psalm 80
- [ ] Psalm 81
- [ ] Psalm 82
- [ ] Psalm 83
- [ ] Psalm 84
- [ ] Psalm 85
- [ ] Psalm 86
- [ ] Psalm 87
- [ ] Psalm 88
- [ ] Psalm 89
- [ ] Psalm 90
- [ ] Psalm 91
- [ ] Psalm 92
- [ ] Psalm 93
- [ ] Psalm 94
- [ ] Psalm 95
- [ ] Psalm 96
- [ ] Psalm 97
- [ ] Psalm 98
- [ ] Psalm 99
- [ ] Psalm 100
- [ ] Psalm 101
- [ ] Psalm 102

- [ ] Psalm 103
- [ ] Psalm 104
- [ ] Psalm 105
- [ ] Psalm 106
- [ ] Psalm 107
- [ ] Psalm 108
- [ ] Psalm 109
- [ ] Psalm 110
- [ ] Psalm 111
- [ ] Psalm 112
- [ ] Psalm 113
- [ ] Psalm 114
- [ ] Psalm 115
- [ ] Psalm 116
- [ ] Psalm 117
- [ ] Psalm 118
- [ ] Psalm 119:1–88
- [ ] Psalm 119:89–176
- [ ] Psalm 120
- [ ] Psalm 121
- [ ] Psalm 122
- [ ] Psalms 123, 124
- [ ] Psalm 125
- [ ] Psalm 126
- [ ] Psalms 127, 128
- [ ] Psalm 129
- [ ] Psalm 130
- [ ] Psalm 131
- [ ] Psalm 132
- [ ] Psalm 133
- [ ] Psalm 134
- [ ] Psalm 135
- [ ] Psalm 136
- [ ] Psalm 137
- [ ] Psalm 138
- [ ] Psalm 139
- [ ] Psalm 140
- [ ] Psalm 141
- [ ] Psalm 142
- [ ] Psalm 143
- [ ] Psalm 144
- [ ] Psalm 145
- [ ] Psalm 146
- [ ] Psalm 147
- [ ] Psalm 148
- [ ] Psalm 149
- [ ] Psalm 150

Bible Reading Plan: Track 2

- ❏ Genesis 1-3
- ❏ Genesis 4-6
- ❏ Genesis 7-9
- ❏ Genesis 10-12
- ❏ Genesis 13-15
- ❏ Genesis 16-18
- ❏ Genesis 19-21
- ❏ Genesis 22-24
- ❏ Genesis 25-27
- ❏ Genesis 28-30
- ❏ Genesis 31-33
- ❏ Genesis 34-36
- ❏ Genesis 37-39
- ❏ Genesis 40-42
- ❏ Genesis 43-45
- ❏ Genesis 46-48
- ❏ Genesis 49-50
- ❏ Exodus 1-3
- ❏ Exodus 4-6
- ❏ Exodus 7-9
- ❏ Exodus 10-12
- ❏ Exodus 13-15
- ❏ Exodus 16-18
- ❏ Exodus 19-21
- ❏ Exodus 22-24
- ❏ Exodus 25-27
- ❏ Exodus 28-30
- ❏ Exodus 31-33
- ❏ Exodus 34-36
- ❏ Exodus 37-40
- ❏ Leviticus 1, 2
- ❏ Leviticus 3, 4
- ❏ Leviticus 5, 6
- ❏ Leviticus 7, 8
- ❏ Leviticus 9
- ❏ Leviticus 10, 11
- ❏ Leviticus 12, 13
- ❏ Leviticus 14, 15
- ❏ Leviticus 16, 17
- ❏ Leviticus 18, 19
- ❏ Leviticus 20, 21
- ❏ Leviticus 22, 23

- ❏ Leviticus 24, 25
- ❏ Leviticus 26, 27
- ❏ Numbers 1-3
- ❏ Numbers 4-6
- ❏ Numbers 7-9
- ❏ Numbers 10-12
- ❏ Numbers 13-15
- ❏ Numbers 16-18
- ❏ Numbers 19-21
- ❏ Numbers 22-24
- ❏ Numbers 25-27
- ❏ Numbers 28-30
- ❏ Numbers 31-33
- ❏ Numbers 34-36
- ❏ Deuteronomy 1-3
- ❏ Deuteronomy 4-6
- ❏ Deuteronomy 7-9
- ❏ Deuteronomy 10-12
- ❏ Deuteronomy 13-15
- ❏ Deuteronomy 16-18
- ❏ Deuteronomy 19-21
- ❏ Deuteronomy 22-24
- ❏ Deuteronomy 25-27
- ❏ Deuteronomy 28-30
- ❏ Deuteronomy 31-34
- ❏ Joshua 1-4
- ❏ Joshua 5-8
- ❏ Joshua 9-12
- ❏ Joshua 13-16
- ❏ Joshua 17-20
- ❏ Joshua 21-24
- ❏ Judges 1-3
- ❏ Judges 4-6
- ❏ Judges 7-9
- ❏ Judges 10-12
- ❏ Judges 13-15
- ❏ Judges 16-18
- ❏ Judges 19-21
- ❏ Ruth 1-4
- ❏ 1 Samuel 1-3
- ❏ 1 Samuel 4-6
- ❏ 1 Samuel 7-9

- ❏ 1 Samuel 10-12
- ❏ 1 Samuel 13-15
- ❏ 1 Samuel 16-18
- ❏ 1 Samuel 19-21
- ❏ 1 Samuel 22-24
- ❏ 1 Samuel 25-27
- ❏ 1 Samuel 28, 29
- ❏ 1 Samuel 30, 31
- ❏ 2 Samuel 1-3
- ❏ 2 Samuel 4-6
- ❏ 2 Samuel 7-9
- ❏ 2 Samuel 10-12
- ❏ 2 Samuel 13-15
- ❏ 2 Samuel 16-18
- ❏ 2 Samuel 19-21
- ❏ 2 Samuel 22-24
- ❏ 1 Kings 1-3
- ❏ 1 Kings 4-6
- ❏ 1 Kings 7-9
- ❏ 1 Kings 10-12
- ❏ 1 Kings 13-15
- ❏ 1 Kings 16-18
- ❏ 1 Kings 19-22
- ❏ 2 Kings 1-3
- ❏ 2 Kings 4-6
- ❏ 2 Kings 7-9
- ❏ 2 Kings 10-12
- ❏ 2 Kings 13-15
- ❏ 2 Kings 16-18
- ❏ 2 Kings 19-21
- ❏ 2 Kings 22-25
- ❏ 1 Chronicles 1-3
- ❏ 1 Chronicles 4-6
- ❏ 1 Chronicles 7-9
- ❏ 1 Chronicles 10-12
- ❏ 1 Chronicles 13-15
- ❏ 1 Chronicles 16-18
- ❏ 1 Chronicles 19-21
- ❏ 1 Chronicles 22-24
- ❏ 1 Chronicles 25-27
- ❏ 1 Chronicles 28, 29
- ❏ 2 Chronicles 1-3

- ❏ 2 Chronicles 4-6
- ❏ 2 Chronicles 7-9
- ❏ 2 Chronicles 10-12
- ❏ 2 Chronicles 13-15
- ❏ 2 Chronicles 16-18
- ❏ 2 Chronicles 19-21
- ❏ 2 Chronicles 22-24
- ❏ 2 Chronicles 25-27
- ❏ 2 Chronicles 28-30
- ❏ 2 Chronicles 31-33
- ❏ 2 Chronicles 34-36
- ❏ Ezra 1-3
- ❏ Ezra 4-6
- ❏ Ezra 7-10
- ❏ Nehemiah 1-3
- ❏ Nehemiah 4-6
- ❏ Nehemiah 7-9
- ❏ Nehemiah 10-13
- ❏ Esther 1-3
- ❏ Esther 4-6
- ❏ Esther 7-10
- ❏ Job 1-3
- ❏ Job 4-6
- ❏ Job 7-9
- ❏ Job 10-12
- ❏ Job 13-15
- ❏ Job 16-18
- ❏ Job 19-21
- ❏ Job 22-24
- ❏ Job 25-27
- ❏ Job 28-30
- ❏ Job 31-33
- ❏ Job 34-36
- ❏ Job 37-39
- ❏ Job 40-42
- ❏ Psalms 1-3
- ❏ Psalms 4-6
- ❏ Psalms 7-9
- ❏ Psalms 10-12
- ❏ Psalms 13-15
- ❏ Psalms 16-18
- ❏ Psalms 19-21

- ❏ Psalms 22-24
- ❏ Psalms 25-27
- ❏ Psalms 28-30
- ❏ Psalms 31-33
- ❏ Psalms 34-36
- ❏ Psalms 37-39
- ❏ Psalms 40-42
- ❏ Psalms 43-45
- ❏ Psalms 46-48
- ❏ Psalms 49-51
- ❏ Psalms 52-54
- ❏ Psalms 55-57
- ❏ Psalms 58-60
- ❏ Psalms 61-63
- ❏ Psalms 64-66
- ❏ Psalms 67-69
- ❏ Psalms 70-72
- ❏ Psalms 73-75
- ❏ Psalms 76-78
- ❏ Psalms 79-81
- ❏ Psalms 82-84
- ❏ Psalms 85-87
- ❏ Psalms 88-90
- ❏ Psalms 91-93
- ❏ Psalms 94-96
- ❏ Psalms 97-100
- ❏ Psalms 101-103
- ❏ Psalms 104-106
- ❏ Psalms 107-109
- ❏ Psalms 110-113
- ❏ Psalms 114-118
- ❏ Psalm 119
- ❏ Psalms 120-123
- ❏ Psalms 124-128
- ❏ Psalms 129-133
- ❏ Psalms 134-138
- ❏ Psalms 139-141
- ❏ Psalms 142-145
- ❏ Psalms 146-150
- ❏ Proverbs 1-3
- ❏ Proverbs 4-6
- ❏ Proverbs 7-9
- ❏ Proverbs 10-12
- ❏ Proverbs 13-15
- ❏ Proverbs 16-18
- ❏ Proverbs 19-21
- ❏ Proverbs 22-24
- ❏ Proverbs 25-27
- ❏ Proverbs 28-31
- ❏ Ecclesiastes 1-4

- ❏ Ecclesiastes 5-8
- ❏ Ecclesiastes 9-12
- ❏ Song of Songs 1-4
- ❏ Song of Songs 5-8
- ❏ Isaiah 1-3
- ❏ Isaiah 4-6
- ❏ Isaiah 7-9
- ❏ Isaiah 10-12
- ❏ Isaiah 13-15
- ❏ Isaiah 16-18
- ❏ Isaiah 19-21
- ❏ Isaiah 22-24
- ❏ Isaiah 25-27
- ❏ Isaiah 28-30
- ❏ Isaiah 31-33
- ❏ Isaiah 34-36
- ❏ Isaiah 37-39
- ❏ Isaiah 40-42
- ❏ Isaiah 43-45
- ❏ Isaiah 46-48
- ❏ Isaiah 49-51
- ❏ Isaiah 52-54
- ❏ Isaiah 55-57
- ❏ Isaiah 58-60
- ❏ Isaiah 61-63
- ❏ Isaiah 64-66
- ❏ Jeremiah 1-3
- ❏ Jeremiah 4-6
- ❏ Jeremiah 7-9
- ❏ Jeremiah 10-12
- ❏ Jeremiah 13-15
- ❏ Jeremiah 16-18
- ❏ Jeremiah 19-21
- ❏ Jeremiah 22-24
- ❏ Jeremiah 25-27
- ❏ Jeremiah 28-30
- ❏ Jeremiah 31-33
- ❏ Jeremiah 34-36
- ❏ Jeremiah 37-39
- ❏ Jeremiah 40-42
- ❏ Jeremiah 43-45
- ❏ Jeremiah 46-48
- ❏ Jeremiah 49-52
- ❏ Lamentations 1-5
- ❏ Ezekiel 1-3
- ❏ Ezekiel 4-6
- ❏ Ezekiel 7-9
- ❏ Ezekiel 10-12
- ❏ Ezekiel 13-15
- ❏ Ezekiel 16-18

- ❏ Ezekiel 19-21
- ❏ Ezekiel 22-24
- ❏ Ezekiel 25-27
- ❏ Ezekiel 28-30
- ❏ Ezekiel 31-33
- ❏ Ezekiel 34-36
- ❏ Ezekiel 37-39
- ❏ Ezekiel 40-42
- ❏ Ezekiel 43-45
- ❏ Ezekiel 46-48
- ❏ Daniel 1-4
- ❏ Daniel 5-8
- ❏ Daniel 9-12
- ❏ Hosea 1-3
- ❏ Hosea 4-7
- ❏ Hosea 8-10
- ❏ Hosea 11-14
- ❏ Joel 1-3
- ❏ Amos 1-3
- ❏ Amos 4-6
- ❏ Amos 7-9
- ❏ Obadiah, Jonah 1-4
- ❏ Micah 1-3
- ❏ Micah 4-7
- ❏ Nahum 1-3
- ❏ Habakkuk 1-3
- ❏ Zephaniah 1-3
- ❏ Haggai 1-2
- ❏ Zechariah 1-4
- ❏ Zechariah 5-9
- ❏ Zechariah 10-14
- ❏ Malachi 1-4
- ❏ Matthew 1-5
- ❏ Matthew 6-10
- ❏ Matthew 11-15
- ❏ Matthew 16-20
- ❏ Matthew 21-25
- ❏ Matthew 26-28
- ❏ Mark 1-5
- ❏ Mark 6-10
- ❏ Mark 11-16
- ❏ Luke 1-5
- ❏ Luke 6-10
- ❏ Luke 11-15
- ❏ Luke 16-20
- ❏ Luke 21-24
- ❏ John 1-4
- ❏ John 5-8
- ❏ John 9-12
- ❏ John 13-16

- ❏ John 17-21
- ❏ Acts 1-3
- ❏ Acts 4-6
- ❏ Acts 7-9
- ❏ Acts 10-12
- ❏ Acts 13-15
- ❏ Acts 16-18
- ❏ Acts 19-22
- ❏ Acts 23-28
- ❏ Romans 1-3
- ❏ Romans 4-6
- ❏ Romans 7-9
- ❏ Romans 10-12
- ❏ Romans 13-16
- ❏ 1 Corinthians 1-3
- ❏ 1 Corinthians 4-6
- ❏ 1 Corinthians 7-9
- ❏ 1 Corinthians 10-12
- ❏ 1 Corinthians 13-16
- ❏ 2 Corinthians 1-4
- ❏ 2 Corinthians 5-8
- ❏ 2 Corinthians 9-13
- ❏ Galatians 1-3
- ❏ Galatians 4-6
- ❏ Ephesians 1-3
- ❏ Ephesians 4-6
- ❏ Philippians 1-4
- ❏ Colossians 1-4
- ❏ 1 Thessalonians 1-5
- ❏ 2 Thessalonians 1-3
- ❏ 1 Timothy 1-6
- ❏ 2 Timothy 1-4
- ❏ Titus 1-3, Philemon
- ❏ Hebrews 1-3
- ❏ Hebrews 4-6
- ❏ Hebrews 7-9
- ❏ Hebrews 10-13
- ❏ James 1-5
- ❏ 1 Peter 1-5
- ❏ 2 Peter 1-3
- ❏ 1 John 1-5
- ❏ 2 John, 3 John, Jude
- ❏ Revelation 1-4
- ❏ Revelation 5-8
- ❏ Revelation 9-12
- ❏ Revelation 13-15
- ❏ Revelation 16-18
- ❏ Revelation 19-22

My Family & Friends

Name

Address

e-mail

Phone

Name

Address

e-mail

Phone

Name

Address

e-mail

Phone

Name

Address

e-mail

Phone

Name

Address

e-mail

Phone

My Family & Friends

Name _____
Address _____
e-mail _____
Phone _____

Name _____
Address _____
e-mail _____
Phone _____

Name _____
Address _____
e-mail _____
Phone _____

Name _____
Address _____
e-mail _____
Phone _____

Name _____
Address _____
e-mail _____
Phone _____

My Family & Friends

Name _____
Address _____
e-mail _____
Phone _____

Name _____
Address _____
e-mail _____
Phone _____

Name _____
Address _____
e-mail _____
Phone _____

Name _____
Address _____
e-mail _____
Phone _____

Name _____
Address _____
e-mail _____
Phone _____